45 Professional Soccer Possession Drills

Top Training Drills From the World's Best Clubs

By Marcus DiBernardo

Table of Contents

Introduction to Possession Training

Coaching possession is about teaching decision-making, guiding players to become problem solvers, helping players understand the importance of positioning and placing players in training sessions that challenge them.

This book contains the best possession drills I have used in my 20+ years of coaching. The training sessions come from Barcelona FC, Everton FC, Arsenal FC, Wigan Athletic, Liverpool FC, Stoke City, Valencia FC, Sporting Lisbon FC, Inter Milan, Ajax FC and many more famous clubs. The drills all have slightly different focal points as I've tried to provide a wide variety of material. Almost all of the drills can be altered and changed to fit your individual needs. It is important to be able to change or alter a drill while still getting out of it what you are looking for. Below are a few ways you can change a possession drill.

Way's To Change or Alter A Drill

- Add or subtract neutral players
- Reduce or enlarge the grid size
- Subtract or add players
- Change the touch restrictions
- Change the direction of the allowed passes (can only pass forward on an angle, no square passes allowed)
- Make new ways to score a point – *Example – 10 passes = 1 goal*

One of the most important aspects of possession training is the number of meaningful touches a player gets. A competitive possession drill should demand players play on the edge of their ability to be successful while receiving many touches. The tempo of the drills should be high, forcing quickness of thought and speed of play. In the modern game, players must be able to play under pressure without losing the ball. Players and teams that can hold the ball under pressure know how to save seconds on the ball. What I mean by that is good players pay attention to the details and simplify the game to save seconds. The difference between losing the ball and retaining the ball can be as simple as passing to your teammate's back foot. Passing to the back foot may have allowed him to escape the defenders pressure. Another example of saving seconds is the coordinated movement between players in possession. Moving into a receiving position at exactly the right time when the player in possession can actually play the pass.

Playing possession soccer is all about positioning and coordinated movement. Without proper positioning keeping the ball would be impossible. Positioning and coordinated movement allows players to create overloads all over the field.

Creating a numerical advantage is critical to unbalancing the opponent, keeping the ball and scoring goals.

Focus on the details when training your team. Make sure you are providing an environment for maximum learning and growth. Pay attention to player's individual technique to save seconds when circulating the ball. There will always be debates about possession soccer and whether controlling possession means winning more games. I personally believe players and teams that possess the ball well have more tools and options to break their opponents down. Possession training makes players well rounded, skillful, composed and gives the ability to find soccer tactical solutions on the field. Passing accuracy is a major statistic that I believe improves with possession training. Teams with higher passing accuracy win more games. Teams with overwhelming possession (over 65%) win more games as well. Of course there are exceptions, but most existing performance data will support these statements. If you are interested in learning about running effective training sessions or building a successful team, club or program be sure to look for my book *"The Method"-The Art of Coaching Soccer at Amazon.com.*

Enjoy the possession drills and feel free to contact me through my blog at www.coachdibernardo.com

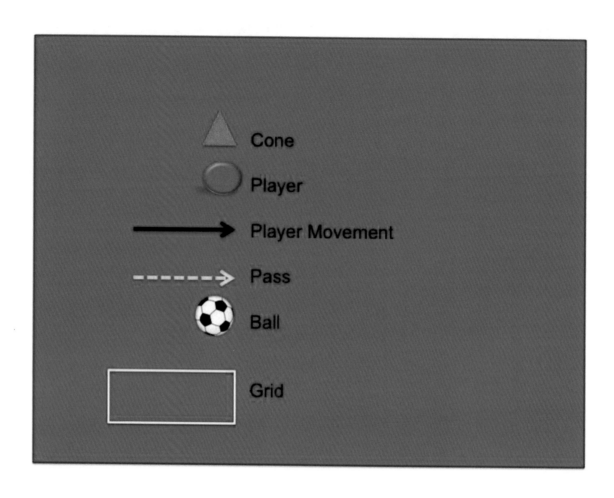

Possession Training Session
Number One
Barcelona Small Sided Possession

Players: 9
Grid: 15x15

Key Points:
This drill ensures players get many meaningful touches on the ball. The object of the drill is to work the ball from one corner diagonally to the other corner. The team in possession will continue to try and work the ball from corner to corner until they lose possession. Once possession is lost, the team who gained possession will try and work ball diagonally to their corner players.
After 3 minutes corner players switch with inside players.
Limit the game to two touches for all players including neutral.
You may only play your teams corner players.

Variations:
Corner players 1-touch only
Neutral 1-touch
Team in possession can't pass back to corner the ball just came from.
Limit the number of passes to get the ball to corner.

Barcelona Small Sided

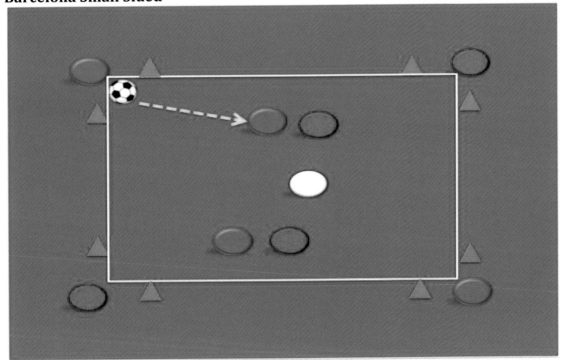

Possession Training Session
Number Two
Bumper Small Sided Possession

Players: 7
Grid: 15x20

Key Points:
2v2+1 in the middle with bumpers that can move up and down the end line.
In order to score teams must use their end line bumper player first. Teams can play backwards and use the opposite teams bumper player for a back pass to keep possession. The neutral player can't score and plays only for the team in possession of the ball. Two-touch is recommended for field players.
Bumper players are limited to 1-touch.
Outside bumpers switch in every 3 minutes.

Variations:
1-touch all players
Scale up the numbers and grid to 3v3+1 and bumpers

Bumper Small Sided

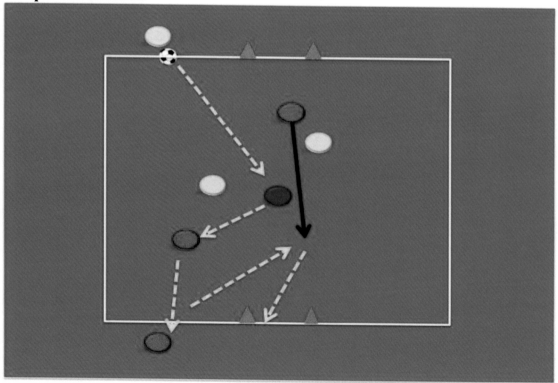

Possession Training Session
Number Three to Five
Speed Possession Progressions

Players: 8
Grid: 20x20

Key Points:
2v2 in the middle with moving neutral players working the lines on the outside.
Neutral players need to be active on the outside and not standing still.
Neutrals can pass to neutrals on the outside.
The middle players can pass to any outside neutral player regardless of the team.
Players can also pass to their teammate in the grid.
The aim is to keep possession as an individual and collectively using your partner and all four outside players. 2-touch for all players.
Speed of play is very important in this exercise. The ball must be moving quickly.

Variations:
Add a neutral player in the middle
Make outside players 1-touch
Make all players 1-touch

Speed Possession

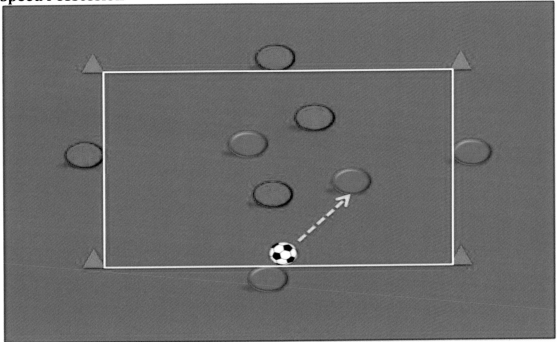

Speed Passing Progression

Players: 16
Grid: 30x30

Key Points:
4v4 in the middle with eight moving neutral players working the lines on the outside.
Neutral players need to be active on the outside and not standing still.
Neutrals can pass to neutrals on the outside.
The middle players can pass to any outside neutral player regardless of their team.
Players can also pass to their teammates in the grid.
The aim is to keep possession as an individual and collectively using your team and all eight outside players. 2-touches for all players.
In this drill use of 1-2 combinations is more available in the middle.
Speed of play is very important in this exercise. The ball must be moving quickly.

Variations:
Add a neutral player in the middle
Make outside players 1-touch
Make all players 1-touch

Speed Passing Progression #1

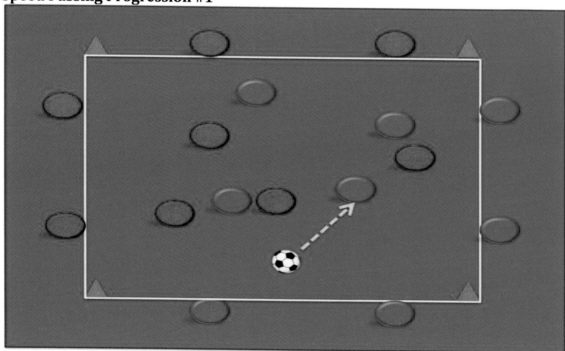

Speed Passing Progression (Cont.)

Players: 16
Grid: 30x30

Key Points:
4v4 in the middle with four of the same team on each end line spread equal distance apart.
Teams play into their end line players on the ground only to score a point.
Players can play backwards to the other teams end line players to keep possession of the ball. This does not count as a point.
Once a team scores a point playing forward into their team's end line players the ball is given to the other team.
The idea of this third progression is to add a direction of play and scoring to the game.
Forward passing is the idea while keeping possession of the ball.
2-touch play to start will enforce the speed of play in possession.

Variations:
Add a neutral player in the middle
Make outside players 1-touch
Make play unlimited for inside players.

Speed Passing Progression #2

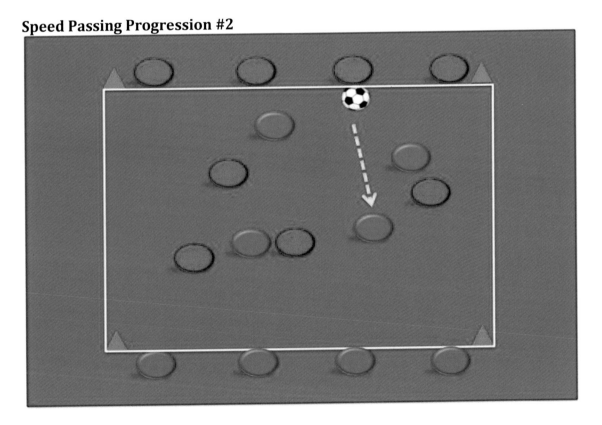

Possession Training Session
Number Six
Outside Switch Possession

Players: 13
Grid: 30x30

Key Points:
4v4+1 in middle with 4 players on the outside. Keep possession with your teammates and the neutral player.
Players can only pass to their own teammate on the outside.
Once the ball is played to the outside player, the player who passed the ball will take the place of the outside player. The outside player now joins the middle.
Keep a fast tempo to the passing. Quick play in small areas is the goal.
Make use of the overload with the neutral player in the middle.
2-touch for all players.

Variations:
Make outside players 1-touch
Make all players 1-touch and add another neutral player
This game is scalable. Add numbers to teams and make grid larger.

Outside Switch Possession

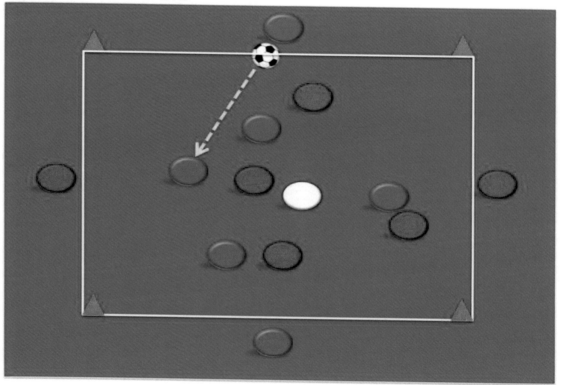

Possession Training Session
Number Seven
Neutral Overload Possession

Players: 14
Grid: 25x40 yards with grid split in half(2 grids of 25x20)

Instructions & Key Points:

4v4 in each grid. The grid with the ball is 4v4+2 neutrals. The grid is split into two with an overload always in the grid with the ball.

After a team completes five passes they can switch play to their team in the opposite grid.

Neutral players will always follow the ball to the next grid when it is switched.

Neutral players after five passes can switch the ball to the other grid as well.

2- touch is recommended to ensure a high tempo of play.

Variations:

Neutral players 1-touch

All players 1-touch

Decrease or increase number of passes allowed before the ball can be switched.

This game is scalable. Add numbers to teams and make grid larger.

Neutral Overload Possession

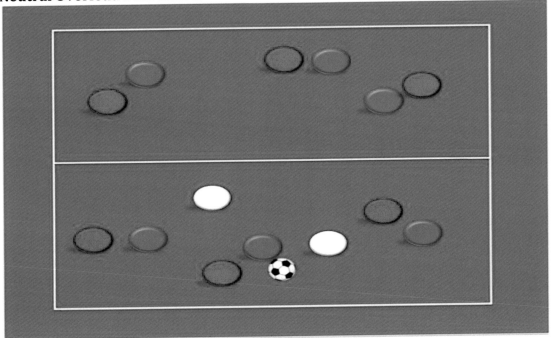

Possession Training Session
Number Eight
Three Box Possession

Players: 11
Grid: Three Connected Grids Each 25x25 yards

Instructions & Key Points:
Play starts in the first box with 5v5+1
After four or more passes the team in possession can play a forward pass into the second box for a teammate to run into. The entire group follows at that point. If the team can make four more passes in the second box they play into the third box. If they make four more consecutive passes in the third box they score a point. If the team in possession in the second or third box loses the ball, start the game over with the other team having possession in one of the end boxes.

Variations:
Add another neutral player
All players 1-touch
Decrease or increase number of passes allowed before the ball can be switched.
This game is scalable. Add numbers to teams and make grid larger.

Three Box Possession

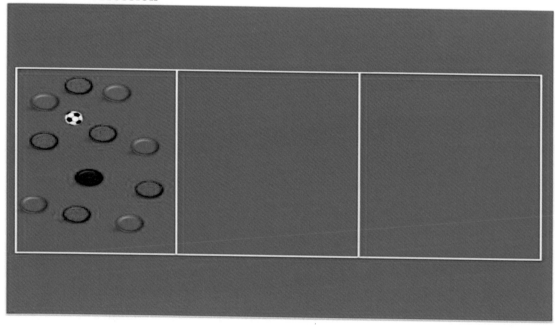

Possession Training Session
Number Nine
Target Man Possession

Players: 13

Grid: Two 25x25 yard grids with a 10 yard wide yard channel between the grids.

Instructions & Key Points:

Play starts in the first box with 5v5+1 in the first grid.

After four or more consecutive passes the team in possession can play a forward pass into the target player in the next grid. Each group will leave one player back as the players follow the pass into the next grid.

The target player holds the ball up and attempts to combine with his team to make four or more passes. The game continues to go back and forth after four or more consecutive passes are made.

Keep play efficient and fast.

Target player must create space and be strong holding the ball up.

Transition must be quick to give the target player immediate support.

Variations:

Add additional neutral player

All players 1-touch

Neutral unlimited touches

Decrease or increase number of passes allowed before the ball can be switched.

Target Man Possession

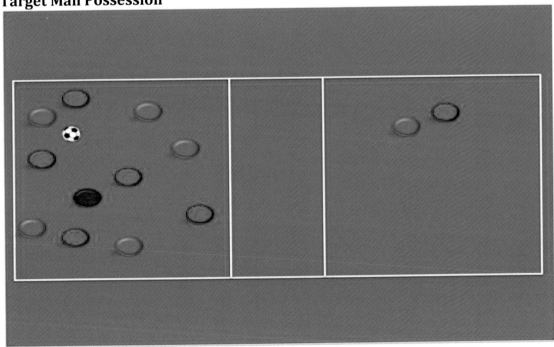

Possession Training Session
Number Ten & Eleven
Three Team Overload Possession

Players: 18
Grid: Two grids each 30x25 yards and one 3-yard wide channel down the middle.

Instructions & Key Points:

Team in middle stays for 3 minutes playing defense. Part One) Defense sends two players for a 6v2 2-touch keep-away game. After five or more consecutive passes the team of six will try to send the ball to the other side of the grid to the other team. The defenders in the middle will try and intercept the ball. If the defenders win the ball, start a new ball on the opposite side with the other team. Rotate the defending team every three minutes. Part Two) Defense sends three players for a 6v3.

Variations:

Add additional neutral player
All players 1-touch
Neutral unlimited touches
Decrease or increase number of passes allowed before the ball can be switched.

Three Team Overload Possession

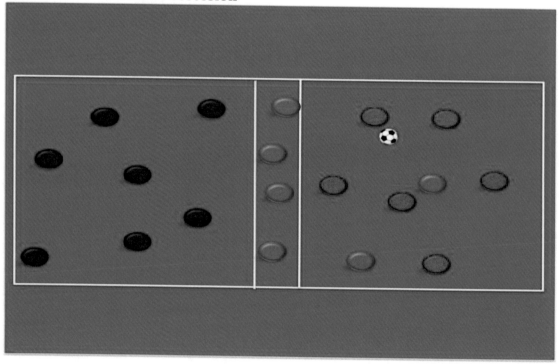

Three Team Overload With Goals

Defending team now sends four players and the remaining two players have to cover the 3 goals in the channel. There is no pass limit anymore. Teams in possession work the ball until a clear shot at goal on the ground presents itself. If the defensive team wins the ball the ball is sent to the opposite side grid. The defensive team switches out every 3 minutes.

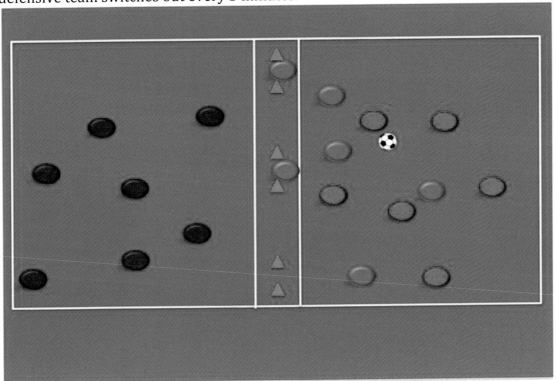

Possession Training Session
Number Twelve
Four Team Possession

Players: 16
Grid: Four grids 15x25 yard lanes

Instructions & Key Points:
4 players per grid. In this diagram the purple team has the ball in grid #3. The red team is allowed to send in one player from each grid that surrounds grid#3. This makes the team in possession which is purple play 4v2 against the red. Purple must complete three passes or more then switch the ball to the other purple team. The red teams will be trying to intercept the ball. When the ball is at the end grids (#1&#4) the defending team will have to send two players in from bordering grid to win the ball.

The game is challenging because players in possession will have defenders coming at them from different angles and over their shoulders.

2-touch is recommended.

Variations:
Unlimited touches or first touch from a switched ball must be 1-touch.
Decrease or increase number of passes allowed before the ball can be switched.

Four Team Possession

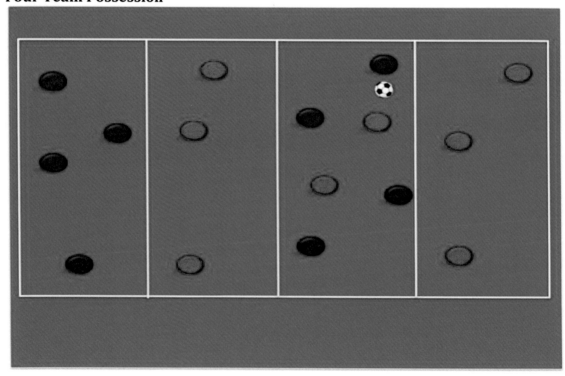

Players: 6
Grid: Two Grids 15x10 yards

Instructions & Key Points:
3v1 in grid#1. Once the defender wins the ball or the ball goes out of play the ball is switched to the opposite grid. The game continues in the other grid 3v1(the player who gave the ball away goes to the other grid as the defender). This game is played 2-touch and can easily be played 1-touch.

3v1 Two Grid Possession

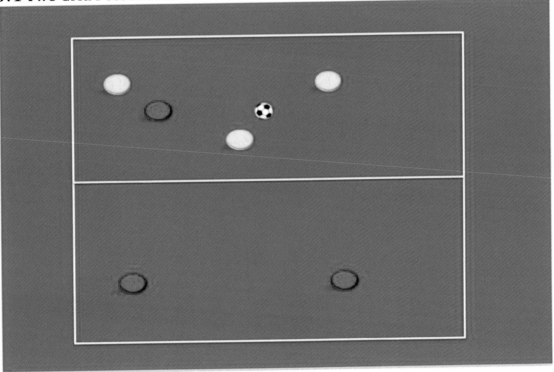

Possession Training Session
Number Fourteen
4v2 Two Grid Possession

Players: 8
Grid: Two Grids 20x15 yards

Instructions & Key Points:

4v2 in grid#1. Once one of the two defenders wins the ball or the ball goes out of play the ball gets switched to the opposite grid. Two players from the team that lost ball will run into the opposite grid as defenders creating a new 4v2. The game is played 2-touch and can easily be played 1-touch. The game should flow well with a high tempo of play.

4v2 Two Grid Possession

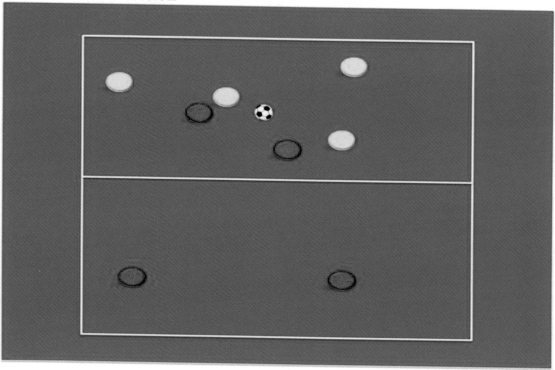

Possession Training Session
Number Fifteen
5v5+4 One-Touch Possession

Players: 14
Grid: 30x30 yards – 10v4

Instructions & Key Points:
Two teams of 5 players & one team of 4 players. The team of 4 players are neutrals and always play with the team in possession. This is a 1-touch only game.
The tempo should be quick with a steady rhythm of play.

Variations:
This game is scalable. Add more players and adjust grid size.
Reduce the # of neutral players to increase difficulty.

5v5+4 One-Touch Possession

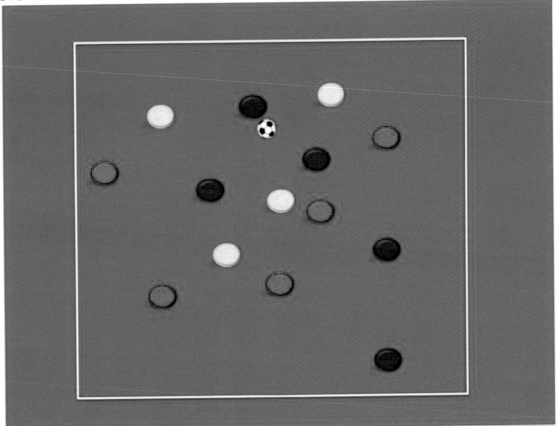

Possession Training Session
Number Sixteen
Three Team Possession

Players: 15
Grid: 40x40 yards

Instructions & Key Points:
Three teams of 5 players each. Two teams play together as one team defends and chases the ball. Whichever team gives away possession they now become the chasers; while the other two teams keep possession together. This game is better 2-touch and then build to 1-touch.
The game should flow well with a high tempo of play.

Variations:
Make the grid larger (45x45) and add 2 goalkeepers. Team in possession can play crosses, shots and different level balls into keepers to save. After the keeper saves the ball they will distribute it to the teams in possession.
This game is scalable. Add more players and adjust grid size.

Three Team Possession

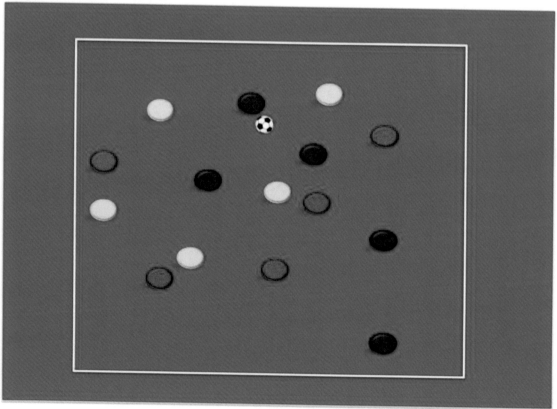

Possession Training Session
Number Seventeen
Switch Goal Possession

Players: 11
Grid: 40x35yards

Instructions & Key Points:
Two teams of 5+1 neutral player that always plays for the team in possession. The neutral player can't score. Goals are positioned wide at the corners of grid. The idea is to attack the open goal. If one goal is defended quickly switch to the open goal. If no goals are open then keep possession of the ball until an opening arises.
Each team has two goals they can score on. Play 2-touch.

Variations:
Can only score after 5 passes
Play 1-touch
This game is scalable. Add more players and adjust grid size.

Three Team Possession

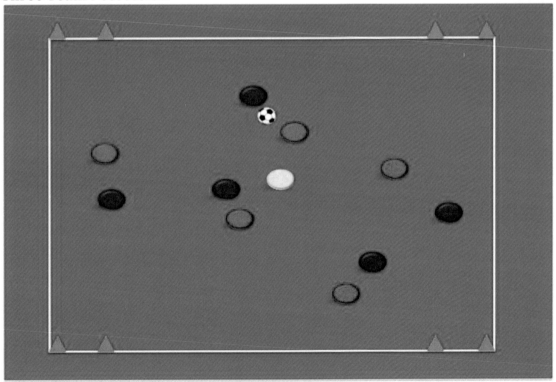

Possession Training Session
Number Eighteen
Switch Goal Overload Possession

Players: 22
Grid: 45x40yards separated in the middle, (two 45x20 grids)

Instructions & Key Points:
Two teams of 5 in each 45x20 grid. Two neutral players in the grid with the ball. Once the team in possession has completed 4 consecutive passes or more they can switch the ball to their teammates in the other grid. Once the ball is switched the team will try to score on one of two wide goals. The neutral players will follow the switched ball and make a 7v5 overload. 2-touch for all players. Red scores on one end and yellow scores on the other end.

Variations:
Allow switching the ball after 3 passes.
Play unlimited touch.

Switch Goal Overload Possession

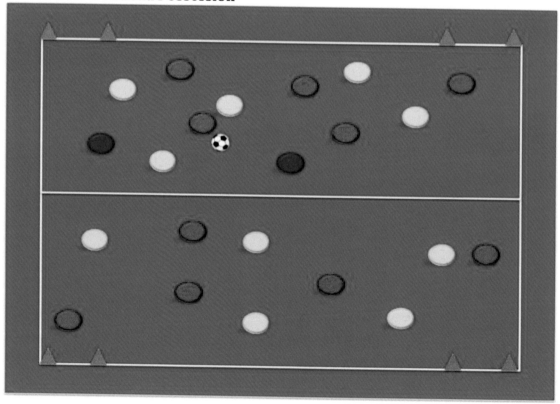

Possession Training Session
Number Nineteen
5v5 Moving Possession

Players: 12
Grid: 2 25x25 yard grids

Instructions & Key Points:
Two teams of 5 with 1 neutral in each grid. After four or more consecutive passes the team can switch the ball to the other grid to the free neutral player. The pass that switches play <u>must be from behind</u> the orange cone in each grid (15 yards in). All players follow to the next grid after the switched pass. This game requires teamwork and communication. Play 2-touch.

Variations:
Allow switching the ball after 3 passes.
Play unlimited touch.

Switch Goal Overload Possession

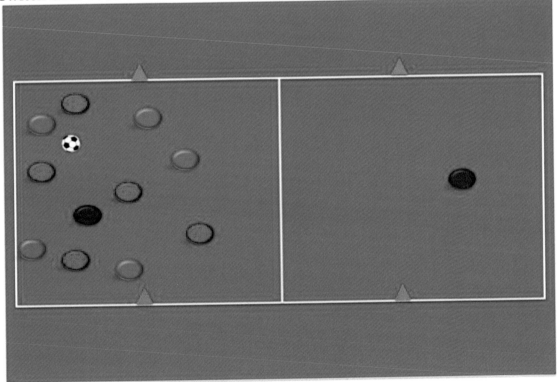

Possession Training Session
Number Twenty
Position Specific Possession

Players: 17
Grid: 30x40yards

Instructions & Key Points:

Two teams of 8 players each with 1 neutral player that plays for the team in possession. Players are set-up in position specific roles. The outside players must stay in their respective zones. The players must only play to the neutral player or players on their team. The objective is to work the ball from the defense through the midfield to the forward. Once the ball goes to the forward the team tries to play the ball backwards through the midfield to the defenders. Establish a good tempo to the drill by playing 2-touch. Players on the outside should move in-support of their team by providing good passing angles. If done properly this drill should be very game realistic.

Variations:

Play with two neutrals
Play unlimited touch

Position Specific Possession

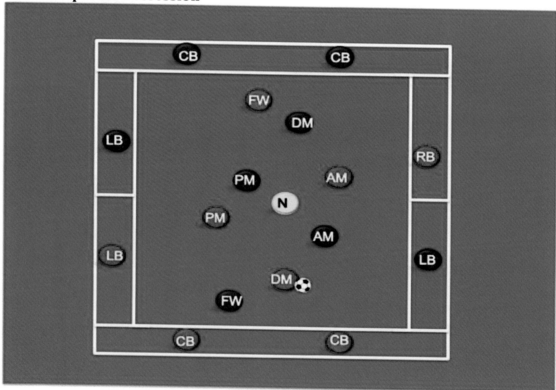

Possession Training Session
Number Twenty-One
No Forward Passing Possession

Players: 22

Grid: 55 yards wide (5 yard channels on each side) x 80yards long
Can play this the width of the penalty box and top of the box to top of the box.

Instructions & Key Points:

Two teams of 8 players and goalkeepers. The rules of the game are as follows. 1) all forward balls must be played on a angle with a 2-touch maximum 2) no square balls all allowed 3) backwards passes must be 1-touch only
4) shots on goal are the only forward straight balls allowed
The game is difficult at first but once players get used to it the results are great to watch. Players will have to support each other in order to be successful. Teams who work in groups of three in possession find success. Players can use outside neutral players who can't be pressured.

Variations:

Play with one neutral in the middle of the field.

No Forward Passing Possession

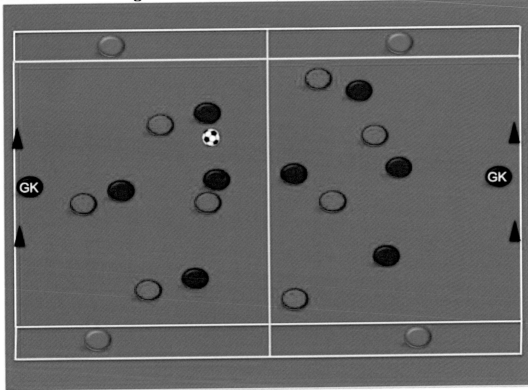

Possession Training Session
Number Twenty-Two
Three Goal Possession

Players: 18
Grid: 80x45yards
Can play this the width of the penalty box and top of the box to top of the box.

Instructions & Key Points:
Two teams of 8 players with two goalkeepers. The regular size goals in the middle are back to back with one keeper guarding each. Each team is going only one direction like a regular soccer game. Teams can score on the big goal facing them or the two smaller goals at the end line. When possession is lost the team must quickly get their defensive shape. 2-touch play. In order to be successful in this game teams must push on and press. The offside rule does apply in this game. That will make the game compact causing teams to press collectively. The pressing team will be open to the counter so there will problems to be solved for both teams. Defending three goals is yet another obstacle to overcome.

Variations:
Unlimited touch
Play with one neutral in the middle of the field.

Three Goal Possession

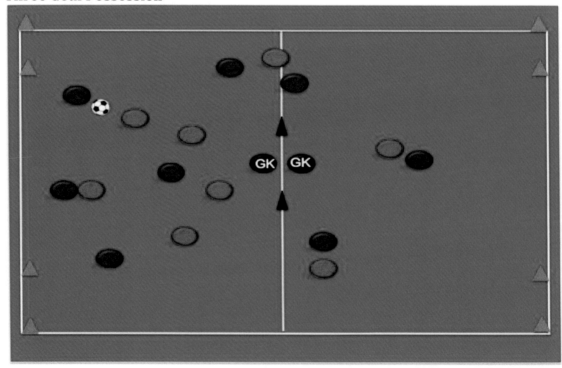

Possession Training Session
Number Twenty-Three
Goalkeeper Switch Possession

Players: 24
Grid: Two grids 35x30 with a 5 yard channel separating the grids

Instructions & Key Points:

Two teams of 10 (split into 5 & 5), 2 neutrals & 2 goalkeepers who operate in the middle channel. The neutrals must play in the zone where the ball is. This will create a 7v5 overload for the team in possession. After 5 consecutive passes or more the ball must be switched through one of the two goalkeepers. Players can put in shots, crosses or passes hit at various levels to challenge the keepers. The keepers will transfer the ball to the opposite grid. The game is played 2-touch and at a high tempo.

Variations:

1-touch
Unlimited touch
Add a third neutral player and game goes 1-touch only

Goalkeeper Switch Possession

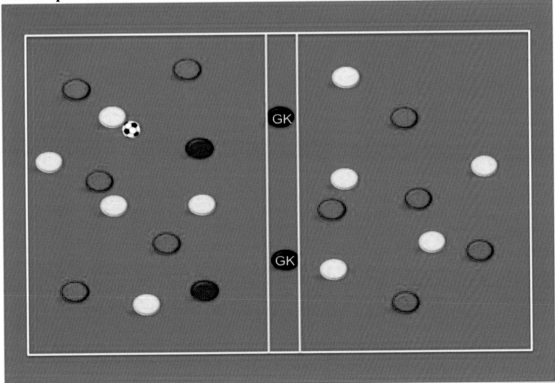

Possession Training Session
Number Twenty-Four
Madrid Possession

Players: 8
Grid: 25x25

Instructions & Key Points:
Two teams of 3 plus 2 neutral players. Neutral players can't score and always play on the team in possession of the ball. 2-touch limit. Red team can only score on the two red goals. Blue team can only score on the two blue goals. The objective is to attack the open goal. If neither goal is open hold possession until an opening is created.

Variations:
Unlimited touch
Vary the size of the grid
Game is scalable if you add players and make grid bigger

Madrid Possession

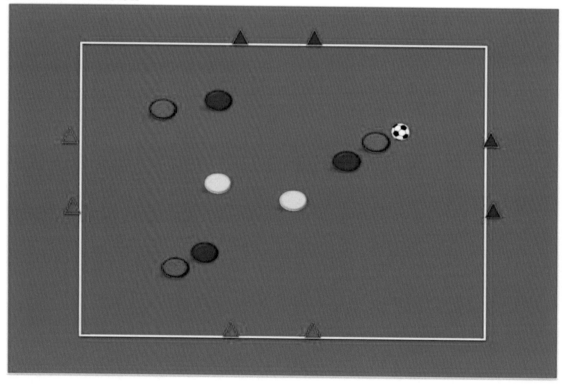

Players: 17
Grid: 45x40

Instructions & Key Points:
Two teams with two regular size goals and two goalkeepers. One team of 8 and another of 7 players. The team with 8 players also uses both goalkeepers in possession to make it 10v7. The team of 10 plays 2-touch maximum. Once the team of 10 loses possession the team of 7 can score on either of the two goals (unlimited touch for team of 7).

Variations:
Add another player to team of 8 so its 11v7 and make it 1-touch.

Valencia Possession

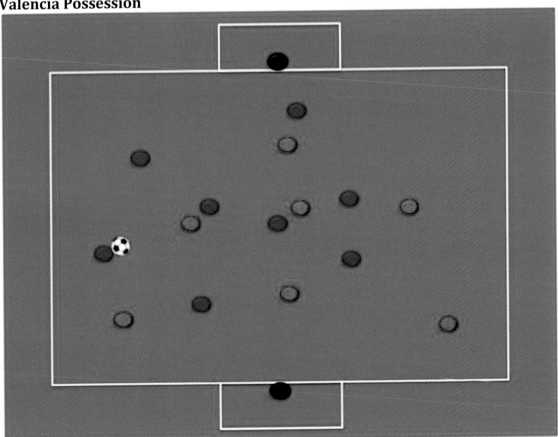

Possession Training Session
Number Twenty-Six
Four Zone Possession

Players: 11
Grid: 45x45 with 4 corner boxes 7x7yards

Instructions & Key Points:
5v5+1. Team must play ball into a corner square to a player on their team. The aim is to play into all four squares consecutively without losing possession. If possession is lost the team must prevent the opponents from playing into all four squares consecutively without losing possession. A point is awarded each time the team plays the ball into all four squares consecutively. Three touch maximum.

Variations:
Add another neutral player.

Four Zone Possession

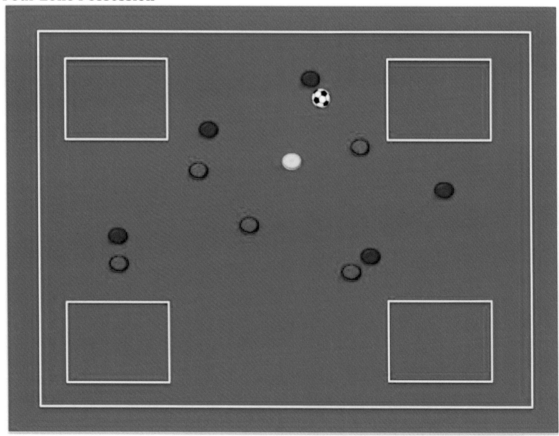

Possession Training Session
Number Twenty-Seven
5v2/8v5 Possession

Players: 13
Grid: 35x35 with 12x12 inside

Instructions & Key Points:
5v2 in 12x12 grid with a 2-touch limit. When the ball is played outside the 12x12 grid or possession is lost, the game opens up into an 8v5 2-touch game in the entire 35x35 grid. Once the team of 5 wins the ball back the game re-starts in the small grid with 5v2. Emphasize that each possession is important and requires work.

Variations:
1 touch
5v2/8v5 Possession

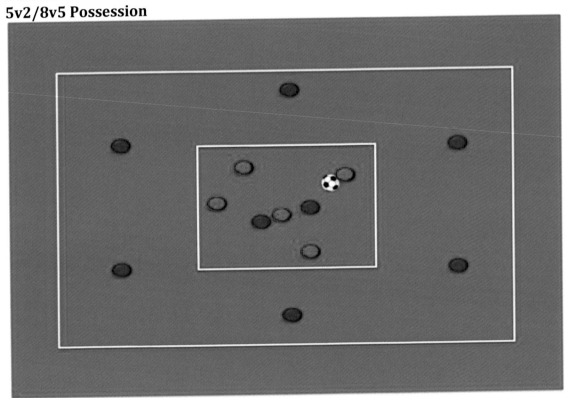

Possession Training Session
Number Twenty-Eight
Arsenal Possession & Finishing

Players: 12
Grid: 25x30

Instructions & Key Points:
6v4 plus 2 keepers. Keepers play on the team of 6 to make it 8v4 in possession. The two players in the middle are limited to 1-touch while outside players and keepers have 2-touches. The team of 4 in the middle get unlimited touches and try to finish on either goal when they win the ball.

Arsenal Possession and Finishing

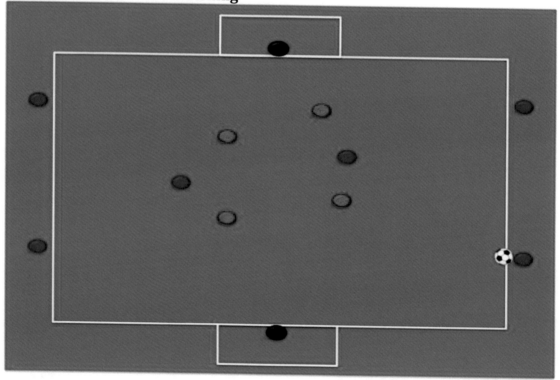

Possession Training Session
Number Twenty-Nine
Half Field High Pressure Possession

Players: 22
Grid: ½ field

Instructions & Key Points:
11v11 (4 players placed in corners)
9v9 play in the field 2-touch maximum possession. The object is for the team in possession to play diagonally across the field to their corner player for a point. The player that plays the ball to the corner player switches positions with him. The team then tries to play back diagonally the other direction to score again. The team defending is trying to press the team in possession creating a turnover. This game is very demanding and requires a high fitness level. Barcelona uses this exercise to train possession under pressure and defensive pressing.

Variations:
1 touch
Add 1-2 neutral field players

1/2 Field High Pressure Possession

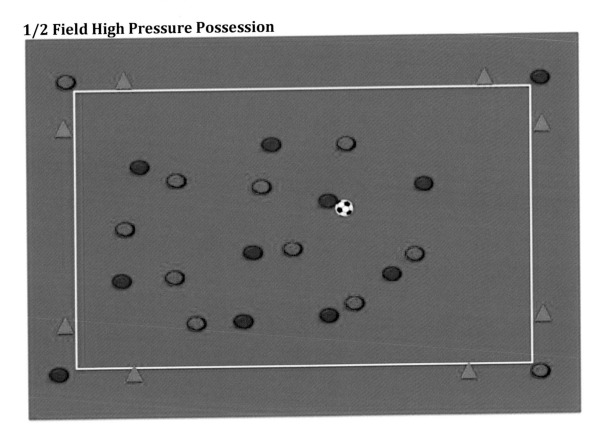

Players: 13
Grid: 50x40

Instructions & Key Points:

7v5 plus a goalkeeper. The team of 8 (7 + keeper) play 2-touch and must work ball out of the back trying to score on one of two wide goals. If the team of 5 gets possession they have five passes to score on the large goal. The objective is to be patient working the ball out of the back using the numerical advantage. The objective of the team of five is to defend as a unit, force a turnover and attack quickly to get a shot off on goal.

Variations:

Unlimited touch

Building From The Back Possession

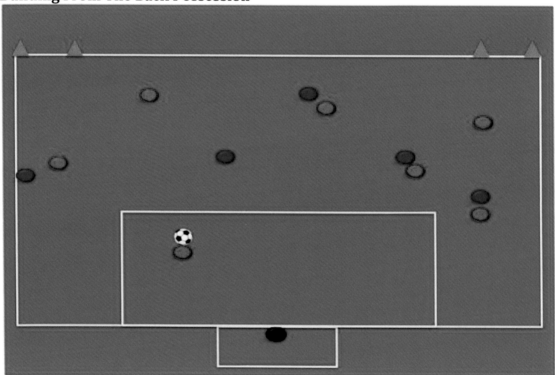

Possession Training Session
Number Thirty-One
Side Bumper Possession & Finish

Players: 20
Grid: 30x25

Instructions & Key Points:
Three teams of 6 players each and keepers. The middle players are all 2-touch and outside players are 1-touch. The idea is to use outside players for 1-2 combinations as teams keep possession and look to finish on their designated goal.

Variations:
All players 1 touch
Unlimited touch for inside players
Add 1-2 field neutral players

Side Bumper Possession & Finish

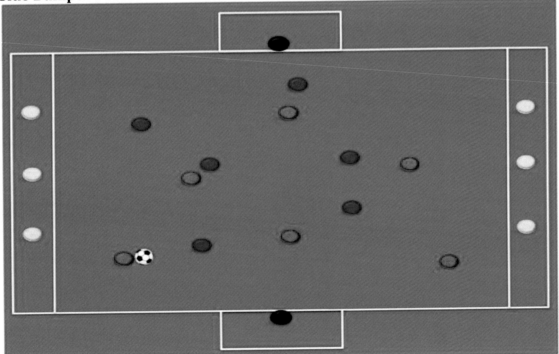

Possession Training Session
Number Thirty-Two
7v4 One-Touch Possession

Players: 12
Grid: 40x36 (split into 2 boxes of 40x18 yards)

Instructions & Key Points:
7v4 with the team of 4 holding the line at the edge of the grid. They are playing with the off sides rule. The team of 7 is 1-touch only. If team of 4 wins the ball the game restarts with ball given back to the team of 7. This possession game helps in unlocking the oppositions back four who are sitting in on the edge of the 18-yard line.

7v4 One-Touch Possession

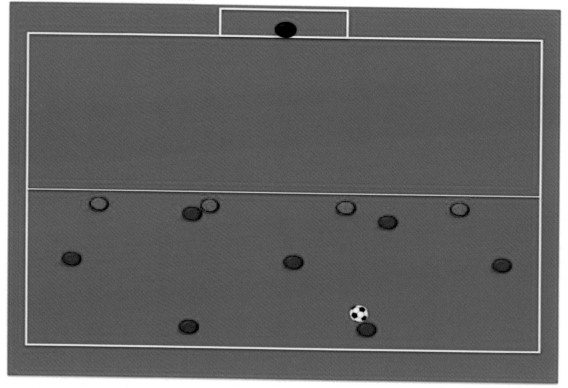

Possession Training Session
Number Thirty-Three
Cross & Possession

Players: 20
Grid: 50x45

Instructions & Key Points:

9v9 plus 2 keepers. The ball must start in the back where it is 4v2 advantage with 3 defenders and the keeper against 2 attackers. The backs must play to a center zone midfielders (2v2 in center zone); the center zone midfielders must play either back or out wide to a winger who is in a wide zone. Once the ball is played wide one middle zone attacker can join the attack with the 2 attackers already in the box, making it 3v3 and the ball out wide ready to be crossed. The game should be played 2-touch on the inside. The progressions are as follows 1) the opposite wide player can join in the attack making it a 4v3 overload for the attacking team 2) the wide player with the ball can dribble inside to the goal and the opposite wide player can come in making it a 5v3 overload in attack. Remove the touch restriction for the last progression.

This game should be fun for the players as the action can become fast and furious. Teams must possess the ball well and be able to use overloads successfully to score.

Cross & Possession

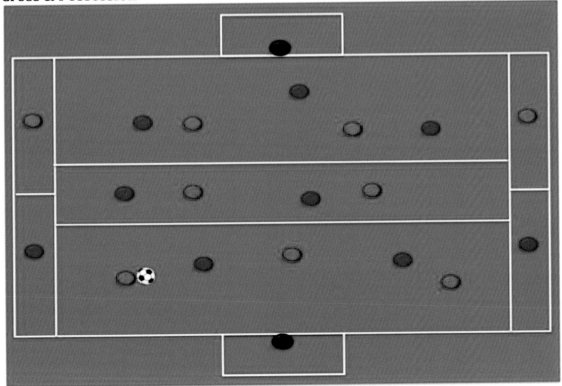

Possession Training Session
Number Thirty-Four
Possession and Shoot

Players: 17
Grid: 45x25

Instructions & Key Points:

5v5+1 and goalkeeper inside box. 5 neutral player's outside box and 1 server with balls. The neutral players can't score. The inside team in possession tries to shoot and score. If they lose possession the team who gains possession must play an outside neutral player before being able to shoot. It is similar to half-court make-it take-it basketball. Play 3-minute games. Rotate teams so every team stays on two times in a row after the first game. The idea is to find small angles to get shots off. If the possibility to shoot is not available use your teammates or neutral players to create 1-2 combinations to open the defense up. This is a very competitive high tempo game that requires quick decisions and combination play.

Possession & Shoot

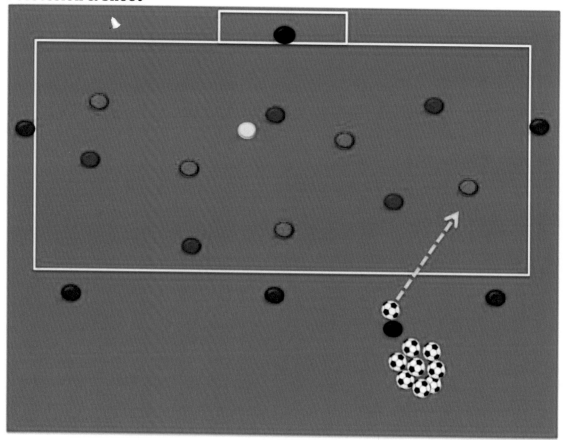

Possession Training Session
Number Thirty-Five
Switch Field Bumper Possession

Players: 11
Grid: 40x30

Instructions & Key Points:

3v3+1 and 4 outside bumpers. The team in possession can use the inside neutral player to help retain possession. Neutral player can't score. In order to score the team in possession must first hit one of their bumper players located at the side of the goal. The bumper player has only one touch to get the ball back to his team who can then score. This game needs to be played at high tempo utilizing change of direction and the overload of 6v3. 2-touch play is recommended.

Variations:

The game is scalable using a larger grid with more numbers.
Add extra neutral and make the game 1-touch

Switch Field Bumper Possession

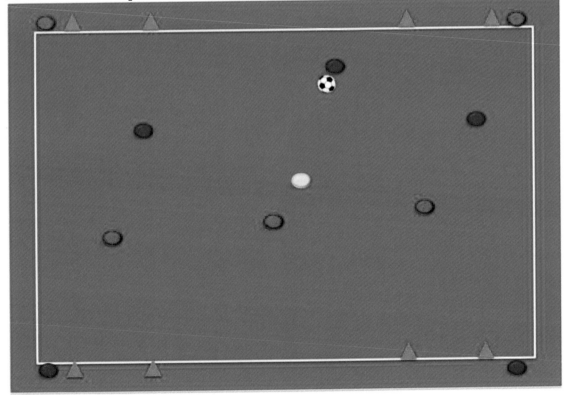

Possession Training Session
Number Thirty-Six
Middle Player Possession

Players: 7
Grid: 15x15

Instructions & Key Points:
5v2. 4 players on the outside can pass to each other and the middle player on their team. The 2 defenders work hard for 90 seconds and then switch out. Play is limited to 2-touch.

Variations:
The game is scalable using a larger grid with more numbers.
2 –touch for outside players and 1-touch inside players.
1-touch outside players and 2-touch inside players.

Middle Player Possession

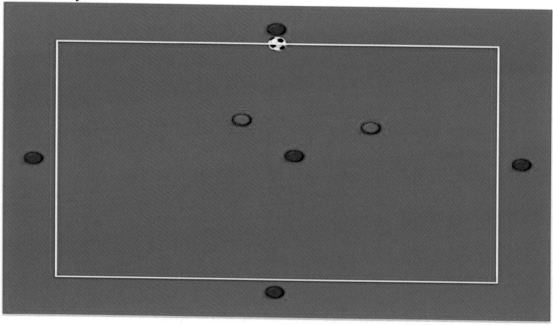

Players: 13
Grid: 30x25

Instructions & Key Points:

9v4. 6 possession players on the outside and three on the inside with four defenders in the middle. Outside players can pass to other outside players and the middle players. Middle players can use the outside players or combine with other inside players. The game is a maximum of 2-touch. If the defenders win the ball they can keep it as the 3 inside blues try and win it back.

Variations:

2 –touch for outside players and 1-touch inside players.
1-touch outside players and 2-touch inside players.

Multiple Middle Player Possession

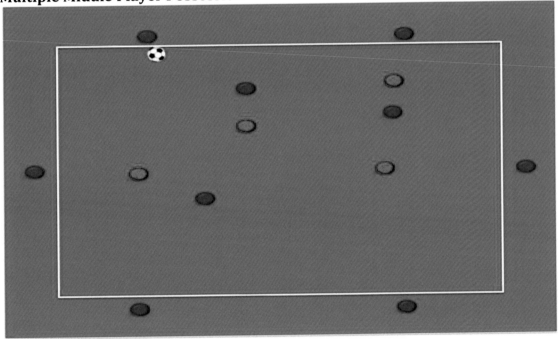

Possession Training Session
Number Thirty-Eight
Overload 2 Goal Possession

Players: 16

Grid: 65x50(channels are 15 yards wide, top field is 30 yards long, bottom field is 20 yards long)

Instructions & Key Points:

One team (Red in this case) is trying to score on the large regular size goal. In order to penetrate the box the red team must play wide to a channel player. They will send another player in after the pass into the channel to make a 2v1 overload. Once the 2v1 overload is established in the channel the goal is to combine and send the ball into the open channel in the final half. If the defender stops the ball into the open channel the players in the channel can always play the ball back into the middle to start play over again.

The objective of the 2v1 overload in the channel is to play a ball into the second half's open channel. One of the 2 players will release and get the ball in the open channel. The red team will then release a midfield player(1 of the 3 in the middle of the field) into the attacking zone making it 3v3 in the middle of the box. The channel player can dribble in or pass into the box and follow. This will create a 4v3 overload in the box as the Red team attempts to finish on goal.

If the purple team intercepts the ball they will attempt to play the ball wide to either channel up the field. They could work it through the middle of the field as part of the build up play. Once the ball is wide in a channel they are allowed to send another player into the channel making it a 2v1 overload to the small goal. This game takes some time for the players to get used to but it really emphasizes the overloads. I like it because the players can clearly see the overloads happening and can get an understanding of how to create them.

Variations:
Remove neutral player.
Make 2-touch for all players.

Overload 2 Goal Possession

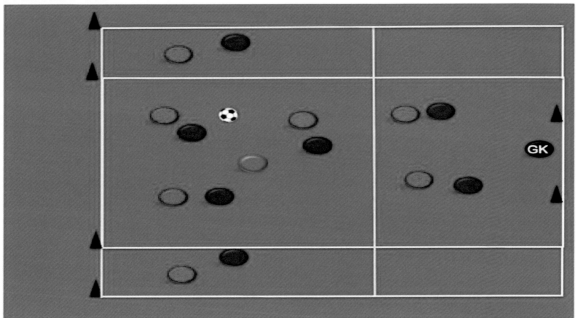

Possession Training Session
Number Thirty-Nine
4v4 Length Possession

Players: 8
Grid: 15x40

Instructions & Key Points:
4v4. Players must find the space in this game. Encourage stretching the game up the field to make it long. Do not play with the offside rule. Players will need to adapt to the new shape and adjust their runs. I first watched the Dutch using this game with their National Youth Teams. It encourages players to play more forward passes and to get into positions of support down field.

Variations:
2 –touch
Add 1 neutral player

4v4 Length Possession

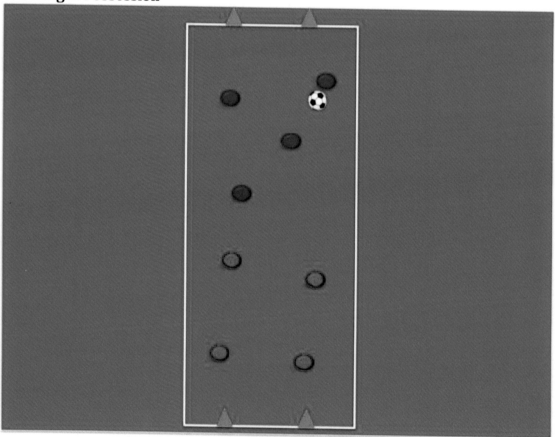

Possession Training Session
Number Forty
Liverpool Shooting & Possession

Players: 13
Grid: 2 penalty boxes on top of each other (45x36yards) with 5-yard sidelines zones.

Instructions & Key Points:
5v5+1(non-shooting team uses the keepers in possession)
One team will be shooting on either regular size goal (blue team). When the blue team has the ball they can use the neutral player to keep the ball and set up a shot but the neutral player can't shoot. If the red team gains possession they can score by passing the ball into a player who is running into one of the side zones. If that player runs into the zone and stops the ball it is a point for red. The goalkeepers play on the red team when in possession of the ball. As soon as blue team recovers the ball they can try and score on either goal. This is a high paced game that works on possession, pressing and shooting. When either team scores the coach will start another ball.

Variations:
Remove the middle neutral player to make it more challenging.
Every 10 passes for the possession team (team that scores in sideline zones) is a goal.

Liverpool Shooting & Possession

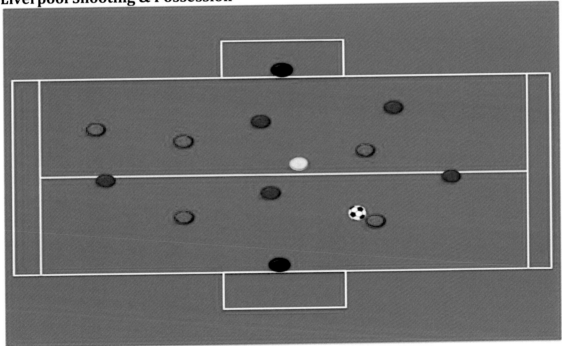

Possession Training Session
Number Forty-One
PSG 11v11 Possession

Players: 22 Players
Grid: Field is 60x75.

Instructions & Key Points:
11v11with full goals and keepers. The two teams play in strict formations (4231/442/433 or whatever formation you use). Play is 5 minutes using 3-touch, 5 minutes 2-touch and 5 minutes 1-touch. The game will be tight and compact on this small field. The tempo usually improves when the touches become less. The next two drills (#42&43) are the progressions to this drill.

PSG 11v11 Possession

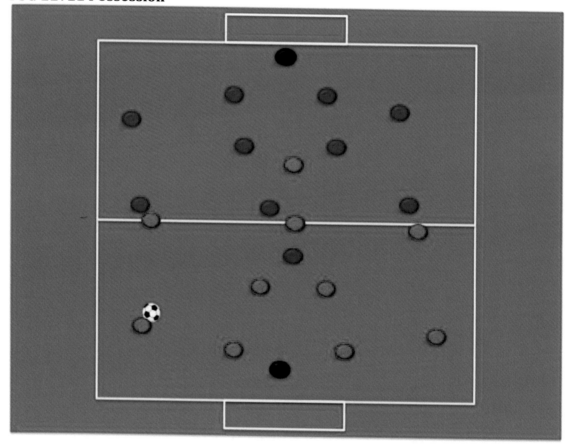

Possession Training Session
Number Forty-Two
PSG 10v10 Zone Possession

Players: 20 Players
Grid: Field is 60x75.

Instructions & Key Points:
10v10 using a set formation (4231/442/433 or whatever formation you use). In order to score the team in possession must pass into a 4-yard end zone to a player who is running into the zone (player can not be standing in the zone waiting for the pass). The game will be tight and compact on this smaller field. Teams will have to work hard to break each other down. The timing of runs into the scoring zones helps collective team movement. Use the same method 5 minutes 3-touch, 5 minutes 2-touch and 5 minutes 1-touch.

PSG 10v10 Zone Possession

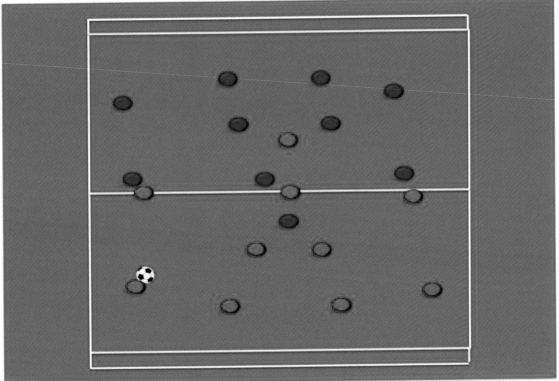

Possession Training Session
Number Forty-Three
PSG 10v11 Possession

Players: 21 Players
Grid: Field is 60x75.

Instructions & Key Points:

10v11 using a set formation (4231/442/433 or whatever formation you use). In order to score the red team in possession must score on the regular goal. The Blue team must pass into a 4-yard end zone to a player who is running into the zone (player can not be standing in the zone waiting for the pass). 5 minutes 3-touch and 5 minutes 2-touch. After 10 minutes have the teams switch ends. The Reds will now be scoring on the zone while the blues will be scoring on the goal.

PSG 10v10 Zone Possession

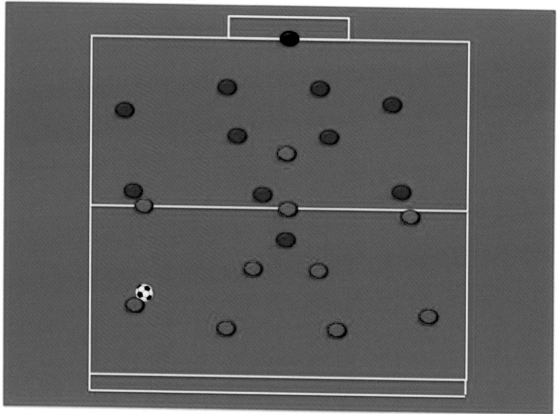

Possession Training Session
Number Forty-Four
Arsenal 10v2 -1Touch Possession

Players: 12 Players
Grid: 10x10

Instructions & Key Points:
10v2. The 2 defenders carry a bib in their hands. If a defender intercepts a pass he will toss the bib to the player gave away possession. Play continues immediately. The entire game is played 1-touch. Players do not make a circle in the grid. They must stay on their toes and are encouraged to move around the grid and be active all the time. This game is used by Arsenal FC.

Arsenal 10v2 1-Touch Possession

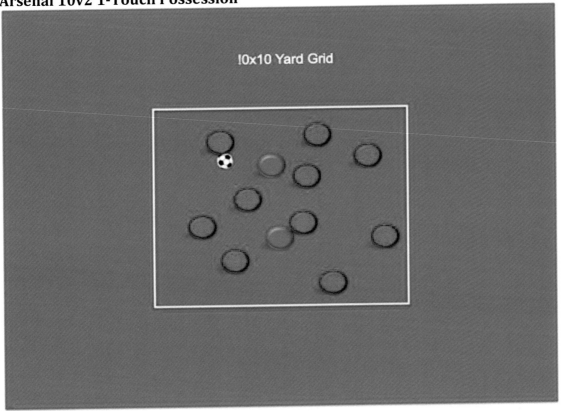

Possession Training Session
Number Forty-Five
Rondo

Players & Grid: 7v2   is used for basic rondo in a 10x10 yard grid. The 10x10 grid is suitable for 5v2 up to 10v2. For smaller numbers like 3v1, 4v1 or 4v2 make the grid a tiny bit smaller. I prefer tighter spaces if the players can handle it. If you see players are having a lot of difficulty keeping the ball make the grid bigger, increase the number of touches allowed, and even eliminate one of the defenders. Players can go outside the grid a foot or so but the idea is to keep the circle shape and not make the circle larger. It may take some time, but eventually players will become more skilled at rondo and keeping rhythm in possession will be possible. Rondo eventually can be played all 1-touch.

Instructions & Key Points Stay on the balls of your feet with open hips ready to receive the ball from both sides and forward while being able to pass the ball to both sides or forward. Always be focused and mentally into the game. Try to get into a high level zone of play and concentration. Begin to think one or two steps ahead of the play. Have fun and bring energy to the group. Let your teammates know when they did well or when they need to pick it up. Clap and shout out the great passes and defensive plays! Speed of play, creativity, teamwork, sound technique and problem solving are all very important in rondo. The importance of keeping possession as an individual and team is the primary objective but look for *passes that split the defenders.* Forward passing is what eventually scores goals. Rondo is a fundamental training drill that should be done every day. Be sure to look for my book "The Science of Rondo" on Amazon.

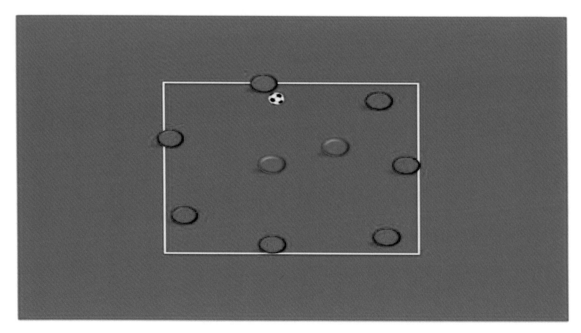

44051529R00031

Made in the USA
Middletown, DE
26 May 2017